VAN BUREN DISTRICT LIBRARY
DECATUR

W9-BCB-032

DISCARDED

TEXAS

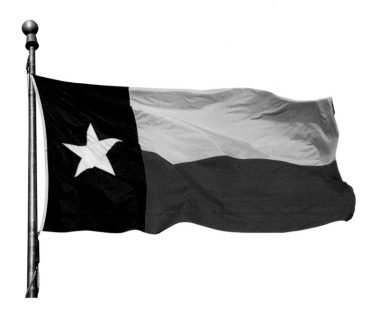

Badges commemorating space shuttle missions

David Crockett

Sam Houston

I LIKE IKE

Presidential campaign button for 1952 election

Settlers in their wagon

American black vulture

American alligator

Monarch butterfly

1900s wide-brimmed
black stetson

Pre-1870s Mexican
felt hat

DK EYEWITNESS BOOKS

TEXAS

Written by
SIMON ADAMS &
DAVID MURDOCH

Longhorn
skull

A Dorling Kindersley Book

J
976.4
Ada

Baseball glove and ball

DK

LONDON, NEW YORK,
MELBOURNE, MUNICH, and DELHI

Editorial director Linda Martin
Art director Simon Webb

**Designed and edited
for Dorling Kindersley by Bookwork
Project editor** Louise Pritchard
Art editors Jill Plank, Kate Mullins
Editor Annabel Blackledge
Picture researcher Alan Plank

Production Jenny Jacoby
DTP designer Siu Yin Ho
Jacket designer Richard Czapnik

This Eyewitness ® Guide has been
conceived by Dorling Kindersley Limited

Published in the United States by
DK Publishing, Inc.
375 Hudson Street
New York, New York 10014

03 04 05 06 07 08 10 9 8 7 6 5 4 3 2 1

Copyright © 2003 Dorling Kindersley Limited

All rights reserved under International and Pan-American Copyright
Conventions. No part of this publication may be reproduced, stored in a
retrieval system, or transmitted in any form or by any means, electronic,
mechanical, photocopying, recording, or otherwise, without the prior
written permission of the copyright owner.
Published in Great Britain by Dorling Kindersley Limited.

A Catalogue-in-Publication record for this book is available
from the Library of Congress.

ISBN 0-789-49745-X

Color reproduction by Colourscan, Singapore
Printed in China
by Toppan Co., (Shenzhen) Ltd.

Rodeo rider
on belt buckle

Republic of Texas $100 bill

Stampede on
the trail

Oil drill
bit

Cowboys' spurs

Confederate
soldier's
cap and
jacket

Mountain
lion

Contents

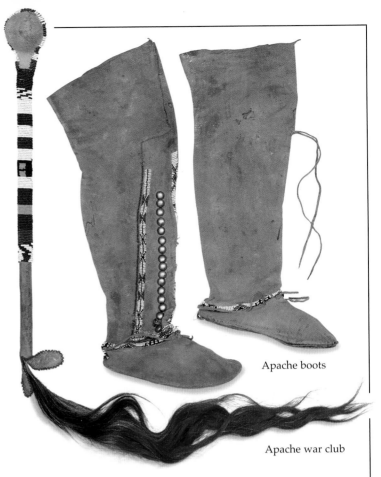

Apache boots

Apache war club

What is Texas?

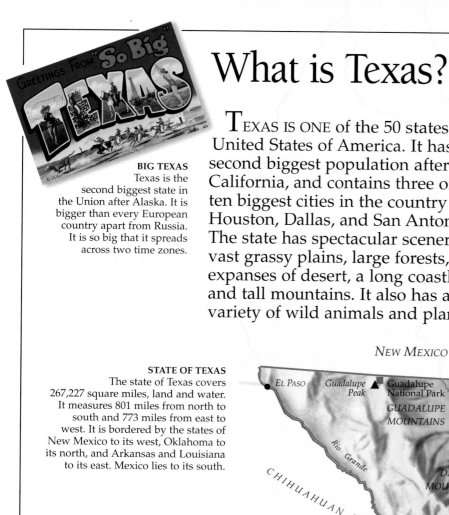

BIG TEXAS
Texas is the second biggest state in the Union after Alaska. It is bigger than every European country apart from Russia. It is so big that it spreads across two time zones.

Texas is one of the 50 states in the United States of America. It has the second biggest population after California, and contains three of the ten biggest cities in the country – Houston, Dallas, and San Antonio. The state has spectacular scenery – vast grassy plains, large forests, wide expanses of desert, a long coastline, and tall mountains. It also has a huge variety of wild animals and plants.

STATE OF TEXAS
The state of Texas covers 267,227 square miles, land and water. It measures 801 miles from north to south and 773 miles from east to west. It is bordered by the states of New Mexico to its west, Oklahoma to its north, and Arkansas and Louisiana to its east. Mexico lies to its south.

THE SIX FLAGS
During its history, six different flags have flown over Texas. They are those of Spain, France, Mexico, the Republic of Texas, and the Confederacy. The sixth flag is the United States Stars and Stripes.

LONE STAR
Texans are proud of their big state and make their many visitors feel very welcome. They call it the Lone Star State, after the flag that was used by the Republic of Texas.

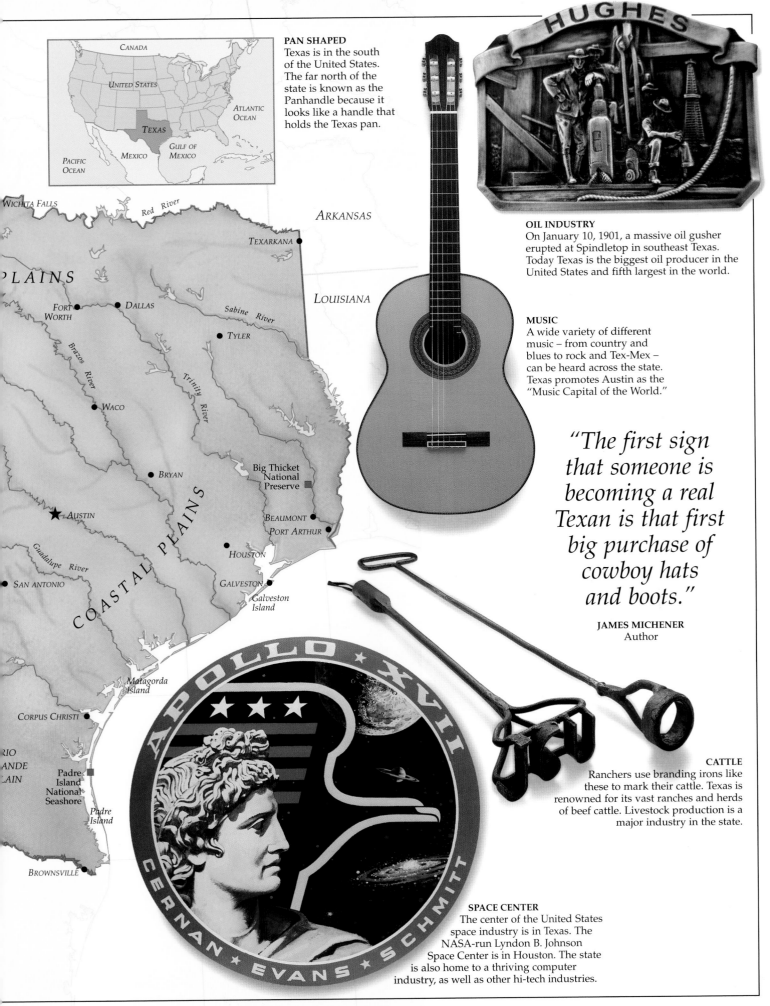

PAN SHAPED
Texas is in the south of the United States. The far north of the state is known as the Panhandle because it looks like a handle that holds the Texas pan.

OIL INDUSTRY
On January 10, 1901, a massive oil gusher erupted at Spindletop in southeast Texas. Today Texas is the biggest oil producer in the United States and fifth largest in the world.

MUSIC
A wide variety of different music – from country and blues to rock and Tex-Mex – can be heard across the state. Texas promotes Austin as the "Music Capital of the World."

"The first sign that someone is becoming a real Texan is that first big purchase of cowboy hats and boots."

JAMES MICHENER
Author

CATTLE
Ranchers use branding irons like these to mark their cattle. Texas is renowned for its vast ranches and herds of beef cattle. Livestock production is a major industry in the state.

SPACE CENTER
The center of the United States space industry is in Texas. The NASA-run Lyndon B. Johnson Space Center is in Houston. The state is also home to a thriving computer industry, as well as other hi-tech industries.

Texas symbols

EVERY STATE in the union has its own symbols, and Texas is no exception. In addition to those shown on this page, Texas has its own state fruit (red grapefruit), vegetable (sweet onion), grass (sideoats grama), reptile (Texas horned lizard), flying mammal (Mexican free-tailed bat), fish (Guadalupe bass), and stone (petrified palmwood). It even has a state seashell, the lightning whelk.

LONE STAR
From 1836 to 1845 Texas was an independent nation. Its flag, featuring the Lone Star, can still be seen across the state.

SUN FLOWERS
The state flower, the bluebonnet, gets its name from its blossoms, which look like blue sunbonnets. In spring, the bluebonnet carpets the fields with its bright blue flowers.

MULTICOLORED PEAR
The state plant is the prickly pear cactus, which grows throughout the west of the state. Every spring and summer it blossoms with yellow, red, orange, or purple flowers.

Monarch butterfly has a wingspan of up to 4in

LONG-DISTANCE FLYER
The monarch is the Texas state insect. It makes a 2000-mile journey south from Canada to Mexico or California for the winter. Females lay their eggs on the way back, many of them in Texas.

Cut topaz and rough topaz crystal

MAMMAL IN A SHELL
The state small mammal is the nine-banded armadillo. It is the size of a small dog and is protected by a bony shell. It uses its keen sense of smell to find food.

TEXAS BLUE
The gemstone topaz is used in jewelry to make rings, necklaces, and brooches. The state mineral is colored blue, but it can occur in yellow, orange, red, green, or colorless.

The nine-banded armadillo is the only armadillo that lives in North America

STATE PRESERVED
The Texas longhorn gets its name from its vast horns. The state's largest mammal became so scarce a century ago that an official state herd was established in 1927.

SWEET NUT
The pecan has been the state tree since 1919. Its nuts are often used in pies, candy, and stuffing. Texas is the largest producer of native pecans.

STATE IMITATOR
The mockingbird is the state bird. It can imitate the calls of other birds in Texas, as well as the whistles and sirens of trains, boats, and automobiles!

Armadillo can be up to 35in long including its tail

Animal can partly roll up for defense

The Central Plains

THE CENTRAL PLAINS of Texas rise from the Grand Prairie in the east to the Rolling Plains in the west. To their north, the Central Plains are bounded by the Red River. To the south of the plains is the Colorado River. Two thin strips of forest, known as the Western and Eastern Cross Timbers, run across the plains. The two biggest cities are Fort Worth and Abilene.

DINOSAUR PRINTS
More than 110 million years ago, dinosaurs like *Tyrannosaurus Rex* roamed Texas. Some of their prints can be seen in the Dinosaur Valley State Park near Glen Rose.

RICH PLAINS
The grasslands of the Central Plains are ideal for raising livestock and for growing cotton, corn, and fruit. Oil rigs dot the landscape because there are rich oil fields beneath the Rolling Plains.

Buffalo grass and oil rig near Ira

BIG EARS
The black-tailed jackrabbit has long, upright ears, which it uses to listen for its enemies. The ears also act as radiators through which the jackrabbit gives off excess body heat.

TOWN LIFE
The black-tailed prairie dog gets it name from the cry or bark it utters when it is alarmed. It eats prairie grasses and lives in large colonies called "towns," hibernating during the winter months.

TREE CLIMBER
The gray fox is unique among foxes in that it can climb trees. It uses its strong, hooked claws to scramble up into the branches.

TWO IN ONE
The prickly poppy is a common sight on the plains. Its leaves look like a thistle's, while the white or yellow scented flowers are poppylike in shape.

EYE GRASS
One of the most common grasses to grow on the plains is blue grama, or mosquito grass. It grows up to 20in tall and has curved seed heads that look like human eyebrows!

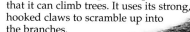

MIGHTY ACORN
The burr oak has the largest acorns of any oak tree in North America – up to 2in long. The tree itself can grow as high as 130ft.

Burr oak leaves

Horizontal pupil suitable for daylight vision

Large ear

SNAKE WRAPPER
Texas is home to more than 100 types of snake. The corn snake first bites and then wraps itself around its prey to suffocate it. Then it eats its meal.

THE BOOMER
The bullfrog is the largest frog in North America. It grows up to 8in long and has legs up to 10in long. Males attract mates with a loud, booming call.

HIGH FLYER
The black vulture has a whitish patch on each wing tip. It spends most of its time soaring high in the sky or perched on dead trees.

The Great Plains

THE GREAT PLAINS of North America stretch from southern Canada down to Mexico. They occupy the western side of Texas from the Panhandle in the north to the Llano Basin and Edwards Plateau in the south. The Caprock Escarpment separates them from the Central Plains to their east. Major cities include Lubbock and Amarillo.

MAKING A SCENE
The fringed poppy mallow adds a splash of color to the plains, as its deep purplish-red flowers stand out against the greens and yellows of the many different grasses.

BEE FOOD
Blue or mealycup sage is a common sight on the Great Plains, where it can grow up to 4ft tall. Its mid-blue flowers produce plenty of nectar, which is attractive to bees.

DEADLY RATTLER
The western diamondback rattlesnake is one of the deadliest snakes in North America. It is the one you are most likely to see in Texas. It grows to more than 5ft long.

NECTAR DRINKER
The cloudless sulfur butterfly lives in the fields and along the roadsides, taking nectar from the flowers that grow here. The male is lemon-yellow, the female yellow or white.

Rattle made up of special scales

Antelope horns and bluebonnets in Texas Hill Country

Agile, catlike body

TRASH RAIDER
The stripy-tailed racoon likes to get its long claws into a trashcan to look for leftover scraps of food. In winter, its thick fur coat helps to keep it warm.

HILL COUNTRY
Edwards Plateau is high and flat, although much of it is so hilly it is called the Texas Hill Country. Lots of wild flowers grow here, and it is home to a variety of animals.

FLOWERS OF FIRE
The blanket flower or firewheel is common throughout Texas and the southern United States. The petals vary in color from deep red to scarlet, with tips of yellow or orange.

FLYING HIGH
The national bird of the United States, the bald eagle is often seen flying high over the Great Plains. When male and female birds court each other, they lock talons and somersault through the air.

Bald eagle egg

Eagles kill prey with their talons

BORROWED BURROW
The burrowing owl does not build a nest. Instead, it takes over a chamber in the old burrow of a ground squirrel or other mammal. Occasionally it will dig its own burrow.

FAST FOOD
Animals such as birds and mice must look out for their lives when a merlin is searching for food. It flies close to the ground and then swoops in for the kill.

Mountains and basins

THE FAR WEST of Texas is an area of high mountains and desert basins. Guadalupe Peak is here. It is one of the Guadalupe Mountains and is the highest point in Texas at 8749ft above sea level. To the east of the mountains is the Chihuahuan Desert. The only sizeable city in this region is El Paso. It is situated just across the Rio Grande from Mexico.

Greetings from EL PASO TEXAS

MOUNTAIN STANDARD TIME
The far west of Texas is in a different time zone to the rest of the state. When it is 7PM in Austin, it is only 6PM in El Paso.

PINK PEST
This beautiful moth is properly called the pink-spotted hawk-moth. It is a pest of the sweet potato, so it is more commonly known in Texas as the sweet potato hornworm.

DAGGERS DRAWN
With its deep orange color and long extensions to its hind wings, the ruddy daggerwing butterfly is easy to spot. It feeds on the nectar of giant milkweed, rotting figs, and other fruits.

Forward-facing eyes allow the hawk to judge depth and distance

LOOKING FOR LUNCH
Distinguished by its red tail, the red-tailed hawk soars high in the sky looking for prey below. Once it sees a mammal, bird, reptile, or large insect, it swoops down to pick up its meal.

FOOD RUN
The roadrunner prefers to run than fly. It has been timed running at up to 15mph in search of insects, lizards, scorpions, and young snakes, or trying to avoid its enemies.

PRICKLY PERCH
The cactus wren loves the hot, dry area of western Texas. It perches on a cactus or hops along the ground looking for insects to eat.

14

El Capitan Ridge

Guadalupe Mountains
National Park

THE INHOSPITABLE WEST
Much of western Texas is desert, and
receives less than 10in of rainfall per
year. The mountains, too, have little
vegetation, making much of the
region inhospitable to animals.

GENTLE SNAKE
The western long-nosed snake is a
gentle species that vibrates its tail
when annoyed. It is cream
underneath, and black
and red on top. It
grows up to
30in long.

Male and
female
bighorn
sheep

BIG HORN
The Texas bighorn sheep was native to
the mountains of west Texas but died
out in the 1950s. Recently, new flocks
have been introduced into the region.

SUN LOVER
The scarlet flowers of
the claret cup cactus
brighten up west
Texas. Also known as
the strawberry or
king's crown cactus,
the claret cup thrives
in hot, dry conditions
and bright sunlight.

DEN BUILDER
The Mexican woodrat drags twigs, stones,
and other material into the cracks of rocks
and boulders to construct its den. It eats
nuts, berries, fungi, and some leaves.

The Coastal Plains

THE COASTAL PLAINS of Texas stretch along the Gulf of Mexico from Louisiana in the east to Mexico in the south. Inland, they reach back about 250 miles to the Red River and the border with Oklahoma. The plains occupy about one-third of Texas. They are very fertile and ideal for farming and ranching. The state capital, Austin, and other major cities, such as San Antonio, Houston, and Dallas lie on the plains.

BAYOU LIFE
The coastline of Texas is indented with bays and slow-moving streams called bayous. Here whooping cranes and other birds make their nests among the reeds. The waters teem with frogs, alligators, turtles, and fish.

Whooping cranes
in Aransas
Wildlife Refuge

SKY WATCH
The turkey vulture soars in the sky in search of food. It uses its sense of smell to find dead animals to eat. It will also kill small animals, such as lizards, or steal other birds' eggs.

MATING RITUALS
To attract a mate, groups of male prairie chickens do a display. They inflate air sacks on their neck and erect the feathers on top of their head. Then they hoot and jump around.

BURROWING BALLOON
The Mexican burrowing frog leaves its underground burrow only to feed or breed. When it is alarmed, the frog inflates its body with air like a balloon.

CACTUS EATER
The collared peccary, or javelina, wanders around in bands of 10 to 25. It spends much of its time eating prickly-pear cactus.

FLYING ZEBRA
The black and white zebra swallowtail butterfly is a familiar sight on the Coastal Plains. It is also known as a kite swallowtail because of its triangular wings and pointed tail.

WEATHER FORECASTER
Green tree frogs often sing together, building up to a huge chorus of sound. They often sing before it rains, which is why many Texans call them the "rain frogs."

COLORFUL DOG
The flowering dogwood tree has white or occasionally pink flowers in March and April. In fall, its leaves turn a beautiful reddish-brown.

BIG THICKET
The Piney Woods of east Texas are part of a large forest that stretches across the southern United States. An area of the woods is now a national preserve called the Big Thicket.

WILD PAINTBRUSH
The Indian paintbrush produces a spectacular display of flowers one year and then virtually none the next. There are nine species of this plant native to Texas, all producing yellow or orange-red flowers.

Tough skin covered with scales

BIG LIZARD
The Spanish called this creature *el lagarto*, "the lizard." It grows up to 16ft long. More than 200,000 alligators live along the Gulf Coast. They eat small mammals, fish, and frogs.

HEAVY OLD TURTLE
The alligator snapping turtle is the largest freshwater turtle in the world. It weighs up to 176lb and has a shell 26in long. It looks very primitive and old.

The Rio Grande

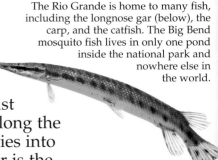

FISHY PLACE
The Rio Grande is home to many fish, including the longnose gar (below), the carp, and the catfish. The Big Bend mosquito fish lives in only one pond inside the national park and nowhere else in the world.

THE RIO GRANDE – known as the Rio Bravo in Mexico – rises 12,000ft up in the Rocky Mountains of Colorado. It flows southeast through Colorado and New Mexico and then along the border between Texas and Mexico until it empties into the Gulf of Mexico. At 1896 miles long, the river is the second longest in the United States, after the Mississippi.

WALL PAINTING
About 4000 years ago, people painted pictures in their caves in the Seminole Canyon. They ground minerals together to make paint, and used plants or their fingers for brushes.

SPEED BIRDS
Peregrine falcons swoop down on other birds in flight at speeds of up to 200mph. They nest on rocky ledges in the cliffs and canyons that line some stretches of the river.

TREE WHISTLER
The black-bellied whistling duck has bright pink legs and feet and a black stomach. It gets its name from the loud, whistling calls it makes.

BEARS IN THE BEND
American black bears live in the mountains in the west of the state, near the Rio Grande. Recently, black bears have also started living again in the Big Bend National Park.

MISTAKEN IDENTITY
The Texas horned lizard is a reptile, but it is often mistaken for an amphibian. It is also called the Texas horned toad.

NIGHT SNACKS
The mountain lion is also known as the puma or cougar. It lives alongside the Rio Grande. It stalks its prey at night and pounces on its victim from an overhanging tree or rock.

SEASONAL CHEER
The Christmas cactus gets its name because its bright red fruits are seen at Christmas time. It is also called the pencil or darning needle cholla because its stems are so thin.

BIG BEND CANYONS
The Rio Grande makes a sharp turn to the north around what is now the Big Bend National Park. Here it flows through three great canyons – the Santa Elena, the Mariscal, and the Boquillas.

Santa Elena Canyon

Climate

Texas is so big that the weather varies considerably from place to place and can change rapidly. Texans joke that if you don't like their weather, stick around for a few minutes as it is sure to change. It is generally mild in winter and hot in summer, wet in the east and dry in the west. The climate is mostly agreeable, but Texas can have heavy snowfalls, hailstorms, tornadoes, and hurricanes.

NORTHERN FRONT
In the winter, cold fronts called "northers" move down suddenly from the north. They bring biting winds and heavy snowfalls. El Paso was engulfed by this blizzard in February 1955.

GIANT HAILSTONES
Hailstones are formed from ice crystals swept up and down inside storm clouds. Most hailstones that fall are about 0.2in across, but in Texas, examples the size of baseballs have been known.

TORNADO ALLEY
Tornadoes, or twisters, are columns of spiraling air that form beneath thunderclouds. They race across the ground at up to 300mph. Texas has about 123 twisters a year, mainly in an area of the Central Plains nicknamed "Tornado Alley."

HURRICANE SEASON
Hurricanes roar across the Gulf of Mexico from June to October. Some hit the coast. In 1900, the city of Galveston was devastated by a hurricane. More than 6000 people died.

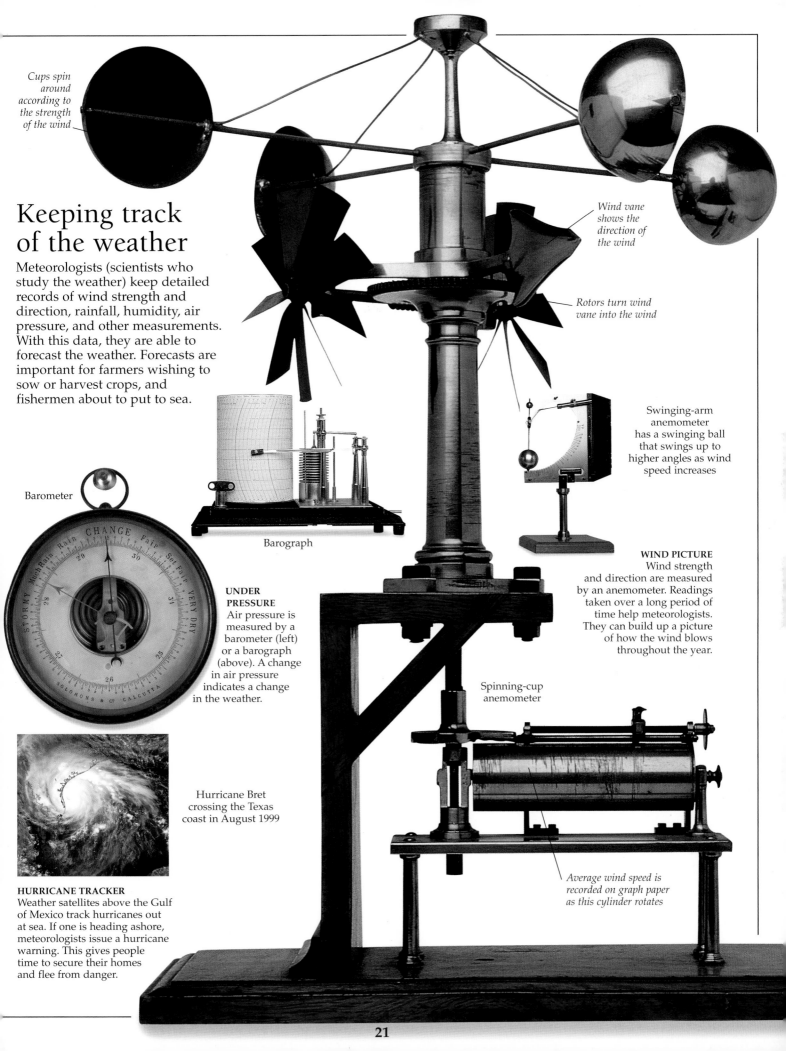

Cups spin around according to the strength of the wind

Keeping track of the weather

Meteorologists (scientists who study the weather) keep detailed records of wind strength and direction, rainfall, humidity, air pressure, and other measurements. With this data, they are able to forecast the weather. Forecasts are important for farmers wishing to sow or harvest crops, and fishermen about to put to sea.

Wind vane shows the direction of the wind

Rotors turn wind vane into the wind

Swinging-arm anemometer has a swinging ball that swings up to higher angles as wind speed increases

Barometer

Barograph

UNDER PRESSURE
Air pressure is measured by a barometer (left) or a barograph (above). A change in air pressure indicates a change in the weather.

WIND PICTURE
Wind strength and direction are measured by an anemometer. Readings taken over a long period of time help meteorologists. They can build up a picture of how the wind blows throughout the year.

Spinning-cup anemometer

Hurricane Bret crossing the Texas coast in August 1999

Average wind speed is recorded on graph paper as this cylinder rotates

HURRICANE TRACKER
Weather satellites above the Gulf of Mexico track hurricanes out at sea. If one is heading ashore, meteorologists issue a hurricane warning. This gives people time to secure their homes and flee from danger.

Austin – capital of Texas

BAT WATCH
Congress Avenue Bridge over the Colorado River in Austin is home to thousands of Mexican free-tailed bats. Every evening, from March to November, the bats fly off in search of food.

In 1839, WORK started on the construction of Austin as the capital of the recently independent Republic of Texas. It sits on the Colorado River roughly in the center of Texas. It has a population of 680,000 and is one of the fastest growing and richest cities in the United States. The state government, the University of Texas, and a thriving computer and music industry are all based here.

"Never in the history of the city, never in the history of the state, was there another such day."

AUSTIN DAILY STATESMAN, MAY 17, 1888
Describing the official dedication day to the new Capitol

Goddess of Liberty stands on top of the dome

The State Capitol and much of the city of Austin is built of pink granite from the Llano Basin

The Texas Capitol covers 3 acres of ground

BIGGER BROTHER
The current State Capitol was built in 1882–88 after the previous one burned down. It was modeled on the United States Capitol in Washington D.C. but is 7ft taller. State senators and representatives sit here to pass laws for the state of Texas.

SMALL BEGINNING
In 1838, the trader Jake Harrell established a settlement that became known as Waterloo. When Mirabeau Lamar became president of the Republic of Texas, he decided to build the new capital city of Texas here.

MAKING HISTORY
M. A. (Ma) Ferguson ran for the office of state governor in 1924. She won the election and became only the second woman governor in United States history. She won again in 1932 before retiring in 1936.

THE NAME OF AUSTIN
The new capital city was named for Stephen Austin. He settled more than 5000 Americans in Texas during the 1820s. He drew this map of the province on a piece of cloth in 1822.

TEXAS FATHER
Stephen Austin played a major role in Texas's fight for independence. He became known as the "Father of Texas."

GOVERNING THE STATE
Every four years, the people of Texas vote for governor. He or she lives in this mansion in Austin just across from the State Capitol. The governor directs the government of Texas, proposing new laws, preparing the annual budget, and many other important tasks.

Native Americans

THE NATIVE AMERICAN peoples in Texas had different ways of life. The Caddo lived in permanent homes. Their word for friend was written by the Spanish as *tejas*, and gave Texas its name. The nomadic Kiowa ranged across the Panhandle. They were allies of the Comanche, who controlled the southern plains. The Lipan Apache fought Texans, but later became their scouts in fighting against other tribes. The Cherokee arrived from the southeast in the 1820s.

LONG-LASTING MISSION
In the 1680s, missionaries brought Piro Indians from New Mexico to found the Socorro Mission in the El Paso valley. The church standing today was begun in 1684, but it was rebuilt twice after floods.

Mano

Metate

CORN GRINDER
This *mano and metate* was used for grinding corn by the Coahuiltecans. This group of peoples lived in South Texas and were nomadic hunters and gatherers.

Caddo

The Caddo lived in the east Texas pine forests. They were the most advanced Native American culture in the region. They were successful farmers and also grew cotton and made fine pottery. They lived in beehive-shaped homes and built temples on raised mounds.

NEW AND OLD
Today, most of the surviving Caddo live in Oklahoma, on land allotted to them by Congress in 1901. They lead a modern lifestyle, but keep their language and traditions alive.

FOOD CROPS
The Caddo grew corn, beans, and squash in clearings made in the forest. The women tended the crops, gathered nuts and fruits, and stored and preserved food like dried corn and smoked meat.

The modern game of lacrosse developed from baggataway

DANGEROUS GAME
The Choctaw began migrating westward in the 1790s and eventually reached Texas. They were friendly with the Caddo and played challenge matches of their ball-game baggataway. Injuries were common.

MANY USES
Buffalo provided the Kiowa not only with meat, but dwellings, clothes, and utensils from their hide, hair and horns. Buffalo skins were also used for paintings.

Migrating buffalo

TRADITIONAL CRAFTS
Today, about 5000 Kiowa live in Oklahoma and earn their living in farming, business, and local industry. They remain proud of their traditions and crafts like beadwork.

Beadwork earrings, headdress, and hair ornaments of traditional Kiowa costume

WOMEN'S WORK
Kiowa women unpacked and packed the tents, called tipis, for every camp, prepared all meals, and made clothing. They carried their babies in a protective cradleboard, a lace-up skin bag on a wooden frame.

Kiowa

The Kiowa were nomads who followed the buffalo herds. They rode far to the north and down to Mexico, as well as widely within Texas. Defeated by the army in 1875, they were moved on to an Oklahoma reservation. After 1900, they quickly began to adapt to mainstream American life.

Continued on next page

SINGLE SIGN
This Apache doll imitates an unmarried woman's hairstyle. Older women taught girls how to be wives and mothers. When a girl was ready for marriage, she ran a ritual race to prove her courage and strength.

FAMILY HOME
During the summer buffalo hunts, Apache families lived in tipis. In winter, they lived in more permanent wooden-framed dwellings covered in hides called wickiups.

Eagle feathers

ELEGANT DESIGN
The Apache did not become skilled potters or weavers. However, they learned to make fine willow-rod baskets and elegant beadwork like this carefully designed pouch.

Clothing made of hide

Cap made of deerskin

Apache

The Apache came to Texas in the 1500s. They formed bands such as the Lipan and the Mescalero. In the 1700s, the Comanche pushed them into west and south Texas. Some Lipan joined the Mescalero, who raided Texas from Mexico until finally defeated in the 1880s. Most Apaches were then moved to reservations.

Tie made of rawhide strip

Metal disc for decoration

SIMPLE HEADGEAR
The Apache sometimes made decorative caps like this one, but they did not wear ceremonial headdresses. Instead, they wore cotton headbands to absorb sweat and protect their heads from the sun.

Glass beads

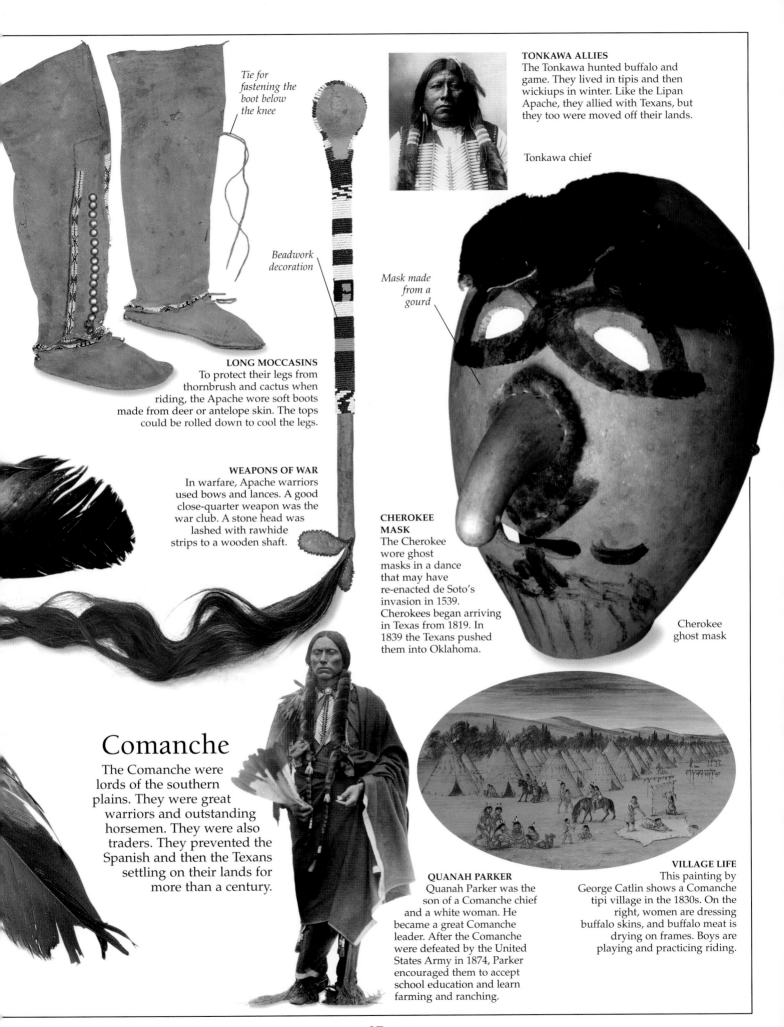

Tie for fastening the boot below the knee

Beadwork decoration

TONKAWA ALLIES
The Tonkawa hunted buffalo and game. They lived in tipis and then wickiups in winter. Like the Lipan Apache, they allied with Texans, but they too were moved off their lands.

Tonkawa chief

Mask made from a gourd

LONG MOCCASINS
To protect their legs from thornbrush and cactus when riding, the Apache wore soft boots made from deer or antelope skin. The tops could be rolled down to cool the legs.

WEAPONS OF WAR
In warfare, Apache warriors used bows and lances. A good close-quarter weapon was the war club. A stone head was lashed with rawhide strips to a wooden shaft.

CHEROKEE MASK
The Cherokee wore ghost masks in a dance that may have re-enacted de Soto's invasion in 1539. Cherokees began arriving in Texas from 1819. In 1839 the Texans pushed them into Oklahoma.

Cherokee ghost mask

Comanche

The Comanche were lords of the southern plains. They were great warriors and outstanding horsemen. They were also traders. They prevented the Spanish and then the Texans settling on their lands for more than a century.

QUANAH PARKER
Quanah Parker was the son of a Comanche chief and a white woman. He became a great Comanche leader. After the Comanche were defeated by the United States Army in 1874, Parker encouraged them to accept school education and learn farming and ranching.

VILLAGE LIFE
This painting by George Catlin shows a Comanche tipi village in the 1830s. On the right, women are dressing buffalo skins, and buffalo meat is drying on frames. Boys are playing and practicing riding.

Exploration of Texas

TEXAS WAS THE FRONTIER for three ambitious powers – Spain, France, and the United States. Spain's conquistadors crisscrossed the Great Plains and the Panhandle from the 1540s to the 1590s, seeking gold. Spanish missionaries opened routes into west and south Texas. In the 1680s, France tried to claim Texas as part of its territory Louisiana, and French traders explored widely. After the United States bought Louisiana from the French in 1803, several expeditions went to the Texas frontier.

FIRST HORSES
There were no horses in Texas until the Spanish brought hardy Andalusians with them to Mexico.

TEXAS TREK
Spanish explorer Álvar Núñez Cabeza de Vaca was shipwrecked on the Texas coast in 1528. He was captured by Native Americans, but six years later he made an epic two-year trek across Texas, eventually arriving in Mexico. His stories led other Spaniards wrongly to believe that a great civilization lay to the north.

De Vaca stranded in the Texas desert, painted by Frederic Remington

18th-century globe showing the Americas

Spanish silver coin with head of Philip II

Crystalline gold nugget

Gold crystals embedded in rock

AMERICAS
In 1494, Spain and Portugal agreed to a deal dividing the world beyond Europe. Spain took the west and gained vast amounts of land including Mexico and Texas.

PRECIOUS METALS
Spaniards had found huge amounts of gold and great silver mines in Mexico and Peru. They went in search of more in Texas but were disappointed to find neither.

Threads of silver crystals

EXPENSES PAID
European monarchs in the 1500s and 1600s always needed gold and silver to finance wars. Conquistadors had to pay the king one-fifth of all wealth they found.

NO SUCH PLACE
In 1540, Francisco Vásquez de Coronado led an expedition to search for the fabled Seven Cities of Cibola. He found only the stone and adobe settlements of the Pueblo peoples.

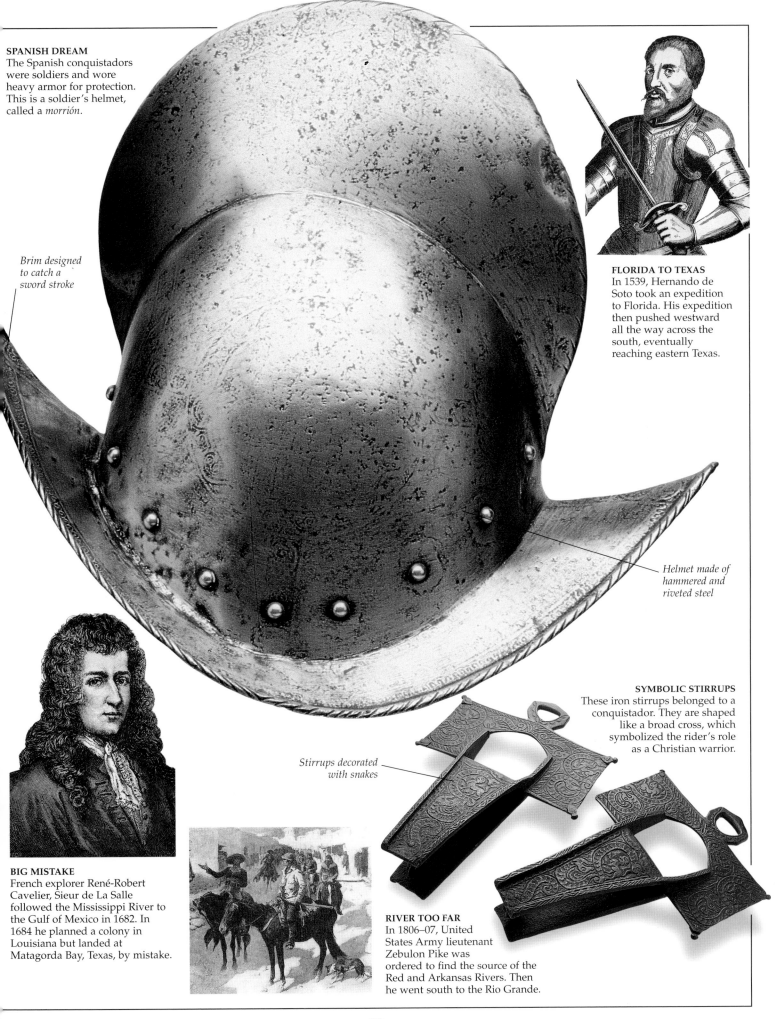

SPANISH DREAM
The Spanish conquistadors were soldiers and wore heavy armor for protection. This is a soldier's helmet, called a *morrión*.

Brim designed to catch a sword stroke

FLORIDA TO TEXAS
In 1539, Hernando de Soto took an expedition to Florida. His expedition then pushed westward all the way across the south, eventually reaching eastern Texas.

Helmet made of hammered and riveted steel

SYMBOLIC STIRRUPS
These iron stirrups belonged to a conquistador. They are shaped like a broad cross, which symbolized the rider's role as a Christian warrior.

Stirrups decorated with snakes

BIG MISTAKE
French explorer René-Robert Cavelier, Sieur de La Salle followed the Mississippi River to the Gulf of Mexico in 1682. In 1684 he planned a colony in Louisiana but landed at Matagorda Bay, Texas, by mistake.

RIVER TOO FAR
In 1806–07, United States Army lieutenant Zebulon Pike was ordered to find the source of the Red and Arkansas Rivers. Then he went south to the Rio Grande.

Settlers in Texas

PEOPLE CAME to Texas seeking new opportunities. Many migrants came from southern states, although soon they came from the Midwest too. A first step was taken by Stephen Austin who set up a colony of nearly 300 families. Other colony organizers, called *empresarios*, followed.

18th-century Spanish coins

SPANISH RULE
Under Spanish rule, foreign trade and immigration were banned. Spanish immigrants were encouraged but few came and the Indian missions mostly failed. In 1820, there were only about 3500 Hispanic inhabitants.

COME TO TEXAS
Advertisements and false rumors claimed settlers would be given free transportation and farming equipment and 40 acres of land.

GRAND RUSH
FOR THE
INDIAN
TERRITORY !
Over 15,000,000 Acres of Land
NOW OPEN FOR SETTLEMENT !
PROCURE A HOME

DANGER AHEAD
People who migrated to Texas and points west had a difficult journey. The dangers they had to face included wild animals, heat, floods, and lack of water.

Pre-1870s Mexican felt hat

MEXICAN TEXANS
Long before settlers arrived in Texas from the United States, Spaniards and Mexicans had been living there. Mexican Texans were called *Tejanos* (male) and *Tejanas* (female).

HORSE POWER
Some settlers who did not need to bring equipment made the journey on horseback.

Compared to the hardships and dangers of the 2000-mile Oregon Trail, the journey to Texas was relatively easy. Across the South, abandoned homes bore the letters *GTT* for "Gone to Texas." By 1830, more than 30,000 settlers had arrived.

INVENTIVE SETTLER
Gail Borden moved to Texas in 1829, became surveyor for the Austin colony, then founded a newspaper. After independence, he became famous for inventing condensed milk.

Hardwood wagon bed with canvas "bonnet"

Iron tires to protect the wooden wheels

Pioneer women usually wore plain, homespun clothing

Pair of Gelderland horses, originally a Dutch breed

PRAIRIE SCHOONER
The best "prairie schooners" were cut-down versions of the Conestoga freight wagon, though many were converted farm wagons, as here. They could be pulled by two or four horses, or four or six oxen, depending on the load.

Continued on next page

Frontier life

Rich land attracted a flood of settlers to Texas. Although three-quarters were Southerners, many also came from Europe, for example Germans, Poles, and Czechs. The population rose from about 212,000 in 1850 to more than 604,000 in 1860. Most Texans lived not on the Western frontier but in the eastern part of the state.

FAMILY STATUE
Pioneer farmers spearheaded settlement of Texas as the frontier moved westward. They aimed to grow cereal crops and raise livestock. This statue of a pioneer family is in Lubbock.

SLOW GROWER
Frontier towns like this one had clapboard-fronted buildings and unpaved streets. Texas industry and business grew very slowly, so towns grew slowly too.

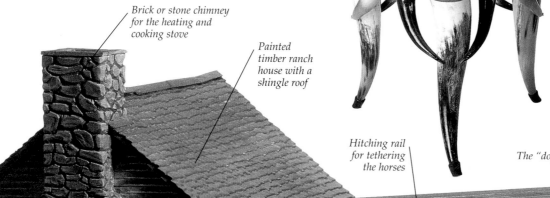

NOTHING WASTED
Settlers had to make much of what they needed themselves. Cattle provided leather, and also tallow for candles. Even the horns could be turned to good use, as in this chair.

PLOWING UNDER GUARD
Texas frontier farmers found Native Americans resisted their advance. Guards were posted to protect workers. The Texas Rangers, and after 1848 the United States Army, gave some protection.

Brick or stone chimney for the heating and cooking stove

Painted timber ranch house with a shingle roof

Hitching rail for tethering the horses

The "dog trot"

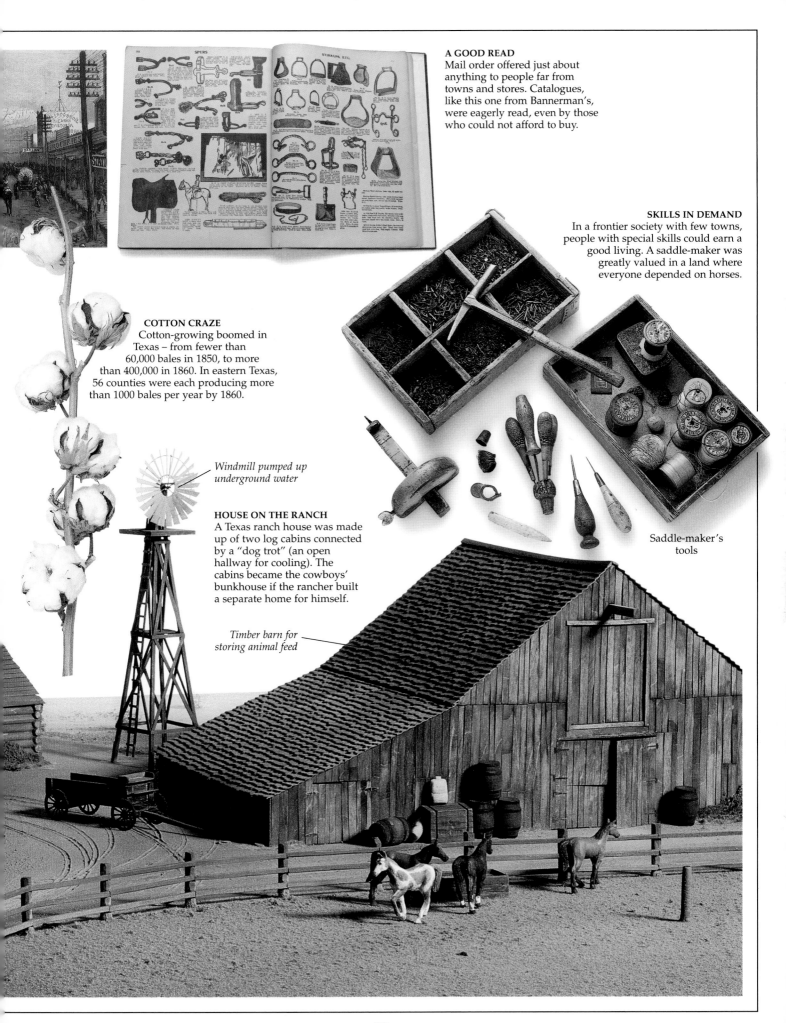

A GOOD READ
Mail order offered just about anything to people far from towns and stores. Catalogues, like this one from Bannerman's, were eagerly read, even by those who could not afford to buy.

SKILLS IN DEMAND
In a frontier society with few towns, people with special skills could earn a good living. A saddle-maker was greatly valued in a land where everyone depended on horses.

COTTON CRAZE
Cotton-growing boomed in Texas – from fewer than 60,000 bales in 1850, to more than 400,000 in 1860. In eastern Texas, 56 counties were each producing more than 1000 bales per year by 1860.

Windmill pumped up underground water

HOUSE ON THE RANCH
A Texas ranch house was made up of two log cabins connected by a "dog trot" (an open hallway for cooling). The cabins became the cowboys' bunkhouse if the rancher built a separate home for himself.

Timber barn for storing animal feed

Saddle-maker's tools

Texas in the early 1800s

Texas Ranger badges

IN 1821, SPAIN agreed to Mexican independence. Mexico abolished slavery, and in 1830, fearing Texas disloyalty, sent troops to Texas and forbade further American immigration. Santa Anna was elected president in 1833. He changed the Mexican constitution and made himself a dictator, so Texas rebelled. Texans, including both Tejanos and Anglos, at first wanted only their rights as Mexican citizens. But Santa Anna invaded, so they declared independence.

MEXICAN FATHER
Miguel Hidalgo was a priest who became known as "the father of Mexican independence." He organized resistance to the Spanish authorities in 1810. His forces were defeated and he was caught and shot.

SENT TO THE FRONTIER
The Texas Rangers were formed in 1835 to defend the frontier. In 1935 they became part of the Texas Department of Public Safety.

Painting of Texas Rangers by Carl von Iwonski

"Remember the Alamo"

Texas voted for independence from Mexico on March 1, 1836. The fate of the Alamo garrison and the massacre of a Texas force that had surrendered at Goliad on March 27 stiffened resistance. At San Jacinto, the Texas battle cry was "Remember the Alamo."

Plaque
commemorating the
Battle of the Alamo

POPULAR POLITICIAN
David Crockett, popular for his frontier humor, made a career as a politician in Tennessee. He left for Texas just in time to join the defenders at the Alamo.

NO SURRENDER
All but one of the Alamo defenders stayed to die with William Travis. Travis was killed early in the final Mexican assault. Jim Bowie and David Crockett died later. The last 11 men were killed defending the chapel.

Santa Anna and (below) his map of the Alamo battlefield

LEFT IN CHARGE
William Travis came to Texas in 1831 and joined those aiming to fight for independence. By 1835, he was in charge of recruitment for the Texas army. He found himself commanding the Alamo when the senior officer took leave.

"I have sustained a continuous bombardment and cannonade for 24 hours . . . I shall never surrender or retreat."

WILLIAM BARRAT TRAVIS
"Letter to the People of Texas and All the Americans in the World"

Fuerte del Alamo

a Entrada
b Habitaciones de Oficiales
c Cuerpo de Guardia
d Comandancia de Artillería
e Cuartel de Artillería
f Cuarteles
g Parque
h Foso interior
i Caballero alto
j Batería a barbeta
k Batería atronada
l Fosos exteriores

VILLITA

San Antonio

BEJAR

de Río Grande

PREPARED FOR BATTLE
Samuel Houston moved to Texas from Tennessee. The Texas Congress appointed him commander of the army when independence was declared. He avoided battles until his army was trained, then crushed the Mexicans at San Jacinto.

FOUR-PRONGED ATTACK
Santa Anna's forces besieged the Alamo for two weeks. The final assault began at dawn on March 6. Santa Anna attacked from all four directions. The defenders retreated to the barracks and chapel, fighting to the last.

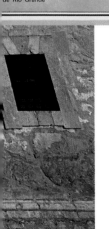

NAMED FOR SOLDIERS
The abandoned mission in San Antonio was occupied in 1803 by Spanish soldiers from Alamo de Parras in Mexico. It was called the Alamo after that. Mexican troops used it as a barracks until forced to surrender to Texans in 1835.

LASTING MONUMENT
The San Jacinto Monument marks the defeat of Mexico on April 21, 1836. Houston's army of 910 men killed 630 Mexicans and captured 730. Only 9 Texans were killed and 30 wounded. Among the prisoners was Santa Anna himself.

The mid 1800s

TEXAS APPLIED FOR ANNEXATION by the United States in 1836, but Congress stalled and the request was withdrawn in 1838. For the nine years of its independence, the republic faced serious problems. There was a constant fear of a new war with Mexico. There was unrest in the army, and government money problems caused concern. Nevertheless, annexation went ahead in 1845, and by 1847 the population had increased to 103,000 with more than 38,000 slaves.

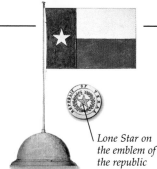

Lone Star on the emblem of the republic

LONE STAR FLAG
The first national flag of the Republic of Texas had a gold star on a blue ground. It was replaced in 1839 by the Lone Star flag.

DRAWING BOUNDARIES
The Texas Congress set the Rio Grande as its southern boundary with Mexico. The eastern border with Louisiana was finally agreed in 1839. Up to 1846, Texas tried to push its western frontier to Santa Fe, New Mexico.

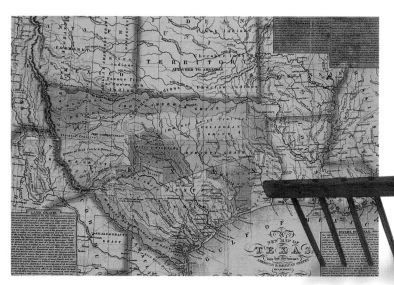

Map of Texas in 1835, just before independence from Mexico

Drag rake for collecting loose stalks left after cutting

GRANDE CITY
El Paso straddled the Rio Grande in far western Texas. At the end of the Mexican War in 1848, the town north of the river became part of the United States.

Barley pitchfork cut from one piece of hardwood

Hand-pushed seed drill for sowing

FARMING SETTLERS
Although cotton was the most profitable crop, growing it required knowledge and skill. Many settlers took up mixed farming instead.

COACH LINK
Early Texas stagecoach lines, carrying mail, passengers, and freight, linked Houston with towns inland. New lines in the 1840s were important in bringing settlers and goods from the Gulf Coast ports to San Antonio.

This 1800s stagecoach could carry nine passengers

Two pairs of cobs connected to the driver through reins

Government issue "redback" $100 note

MEXICAN WAR
After Texas was annexed to the United States, war broke out with Mexico. General Zachary Taylor commanded the United States Army. He defeated the Mexican forces in several battles.

Grain crops were hand-harvested with a sickle and scythe

Cut cereals were stacked in sheaves to dry out

Zachary Taylor in the uniform of Major-General

HENRY CLAY, AND A PROTECTIVE TARIFF.
NO ANNEXATION OF TEXAS!
No Extension of Slavery!!
With Henry Clay
We'll win the day,
And Home Industry defend;
With Polk and Dallas
We'll to the gallows
Free Trade and Texas send.

DEVALUED CURRENCY
The republic first issued paper money in 1837. A new issue of banknotes in 1839, called "redbacks," totaled more than $3.5 million. But Texans did not trust redbacks, so their value fell to 2 cents for each dollar.

1844 presidential campaign ribbon

VOTES IN FAVOR
Whether to annex Texas was the burning issue of the 1844 United States presidential election. Whig candidate Henry Clay was opposed, but Democrat James Polk, who won the election, was strongly in favor.

The late 1800s

UNCLE TOM'S CABIN
The novel *Uncle Tom's Cabin* was published in 1852. Written by Harriet Beecher Stowe, it highlighted the wrongs of slavery and helped to strengthen antislavery feelings.

In 1860, AFRICAN-AMERICAN slavery existed in all the southern states. Only one-quarter of Texans owned slaves, but like most Southerners they saw slavery as part of their way of life and feared its abolition. In the 1860 election, Abraham Lincoln promised not to abolish slavery but only to prevent its spread to the new territories. Southerners did not believe him, and most states in the South decided to form their own nation. It was called the Confederate States of America. Civil War broke out in 1861.

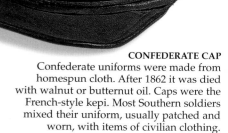

CONFEDERATE CAP
Confederate uniforms were made from homespun cloth. After 1862 it was died with walnut or butternut oil. Caps were the French-style kepi. Most Southern soldiers mixed their uniform, usually patched and worn, with items of civilian clothing.

DIVIDED COUNTRY
In 1860, 15 out of 33 states were slave states. Eleven of these left the Union and became the Confederate States of America. Sam Houston, Texas Governor, was a strong Unionist but Texas joined the Confederacy in February 1861.

CONFEDERACY

UNION

BORDER STATES

Confederate soldier

Union soldier

Muzzle-loading rifle

The "Stars and Bars," used until 1863

Flag of Company F, 1st Texas Cavalry, formerly Ware's Partisan Rangers

FLYING THE FLAGS
The first official flag of the Confederacy was the "Stars and Bars." Extra stars were added as states joined the original seven. The Confederate Battle Flag, with a St. Andrew's cross was used throughout the war.

Battle flag of 2nd battalion, Hilliard's Alabama Legion

SUPERIOR SUPPLIES
The war was won by the Union largely because it had the industries to arm and supply its troops. Unlike the South, the North had more factories to provide arms, ammunition, and uniforms.

ABRAHAM LINCOLN
Although Lincoln freed the slaves by proclamation in 1863, he fought the war to save the Union. Union armies finally forced the surrender of the Confederacy in April 1865.

Image of Abraham Lincoln

"Greenbacks," which were similar to these modern bills, were introduced during Lincoln's presidency

LIFE AND DEATH
Army surgeons worked desperately to save lives but they lacked modern equipment, drugs, and medical knowledge. More than 620,000 men died, half from disease, and more than 50,000 had arms or legs amputated.

Civil War pharmacy chest

Fine scales for weighing tiny quantities of medication

Pestle and mortar for grinding drugs for pills, rolled by hand

Glass bottles for medicine

Containers for burning spirit for sterilizing surgical instruments

Polished hardwood container for pills

Camp desk

WRITTEN RECORDS
The two armies needed written orders, lists of supplies, and proper records. Clerks and officers used laptop desks, made to fold into a flat box. Most soldiers also tried to write home to their families.

Portable inkwell with screw top

RITTER'S PATENT
PORTABLE WRITING DESK
PORT-FOLIO, WORK-BOX, DRESSING-CASE & CHEQUER BOARD

Pen with steel tip

HENRY OSSIAN FLIPPER
It wasn't until 1877 that the first African-American graduated from West Point military academy. Texan Henry Ossian Flipper served in the West as a lieutenant in the 10th Cavalry. He suffered persecution from white officers until dismissed in 1883.

Life as a cowboy

T HE COWBOYS' heydey lasted only for the 20 years of open-range ranching, 1866–86. Their work was hard and badly paid. The first cowboys were Texans. Later some came from the South, the Midwest, and even from Europe. Mexican-American cowboys were common, and about one-fifth were African-Americans. By the 1890s, the cowboys' way of life was disappearing. Then it suddenly seemed romantic and exciting.

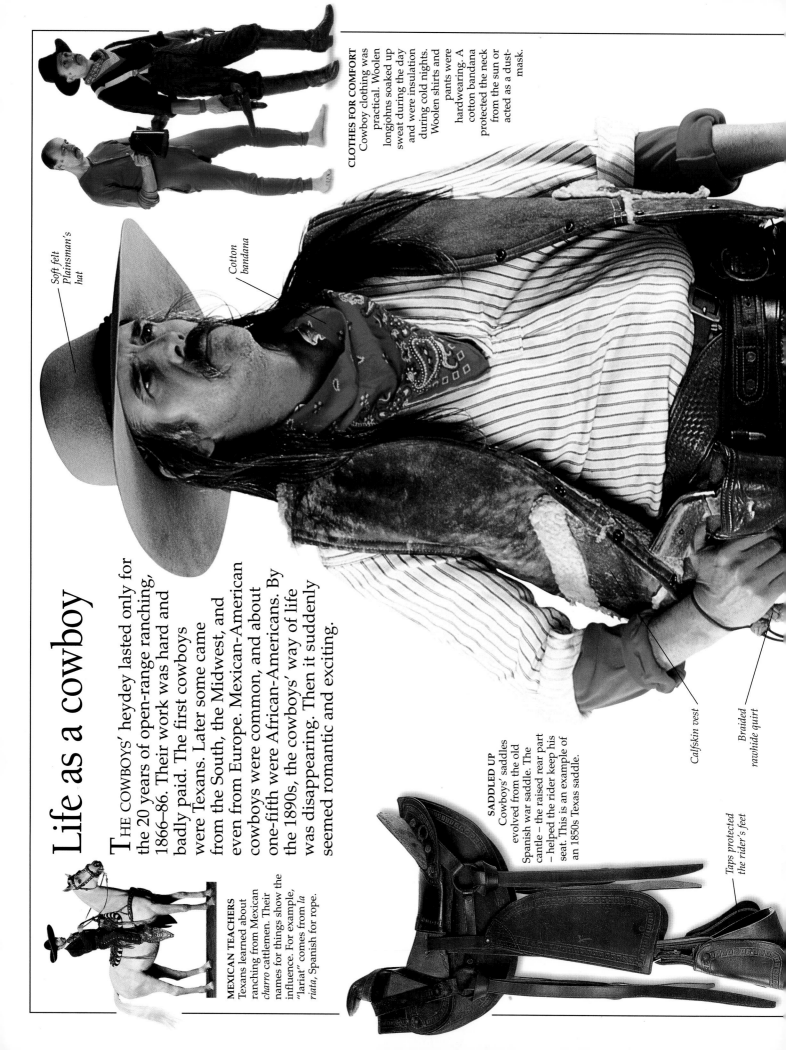

CLOTHES FOR COMFORT
Cowboy clothing was practical. Woolen longjohns soaked up sweat during the day and were insulation during cold nights. Woolen shirts and pants were hardwearing. A cotton bandana protected the neck from the sun or acted as a dust-mask.

Soft felt Plainsman's hat

Cotton bandana

Calfskin vest

Braided rawhide quirt

MEXICAN TEACHERS
Texans learned about ranching from Mexican *charro* cattlemen. Their names for things show the influence. For example, "lariat" comes from *la riata*, Spanish for rope.

SADDLED UP
Cowboys' saddles evolved from the old Spanish war saddle. The cantle – the raised rear part – helped the rider keep his seat. This is an example of an 1850s Texas saddle.

Taps protected the rider's feet

Lariat

TRUE COWBOY
A Texas cowboy's work was brutally hard, often monotonous, and sometimes very dangerous. The work required courage and endurance and a cowboy took pride in his lifestyle.

Silver conchas stopped the ties being pulled through

Rowel spur

Underslung heel

Batwing chaps were tied at the back of the leg

NO JOB FOR A WOMAN
Women on the 19th-century Texas frontier were homemakers, teachers, even saloon girls. Cowgirls were unknown. Only in the 20th century did conventions change so that women could work alongside cowboys.

LEG PROTECTION
Cowboy boots were tall to protect the legs. High heels prevented the feet from slipping through the stirrups and could be dug into the ground when roping on foot.

SPURRED ON
Cowboys did not groom their horses, so used spurs to prick through the matted hair. Rowel spurs look cruel but were usually filed blunt.

On the range

OPEN-RANGE ranching took off in Texas after the Civil War, when eastern cities' demand for beef made big profits possible. Trails linked Texas ranges with Kansas railheads, so cattle could be sent to the big meat-packing centers like Chicago. The beef "bonanza" lasted only 20 years. It was ended by overstocking, falling prices, fencing the range, and the terrible winter of 1886–87.

MIXED STOCK
The Texas longhorn was a mixture of the descendants of Spanish cattle and English stock brought from the Midwest. Millions of longhorns had bred untended in the wild during the Civil War.

KINGSVILLE
HOME OF THE WORLD FAMOUS
KING RANCH

KING RANCH
Richard King began to set up the King Ranch in 1852. Today, with 825,000 acres, it is the largest cattle ranch in the world. It is famous for its Brahma and St. Gertrudis cattle.

Kerosene lamp

CHUCK WAGON
Life on the trail was hard work. The cowboys had to keep the herd together, cross rivers, and prevent stampedes. They relied on the camp cook for hot meals. His chuck wagon was kitchen, larder, and equipment store.

Iron skillet for frying bacon and making sourdough bread

LONG TRAIL
It took three months to drive cattle the 1000 miles of the Chisholm Trail from south Texas to Abilene, Kansas. More than 1.5 million cattle took this trail between 1867 and 1870.

A longhorn's horns might measure 5ft from tip to tip

HARDY BEASTS
Longhorns were half-wild, mean-tempered animals, but they were hardy. They survived easily on the sparse grass of the plains. Their long legs and tough hoofs allowed them to cope well with the trail.

Cook pan for beans and stews

"Wreck pan" for dirty dishes

WATER SUPPLY
On the trail, thirst was a constant threat. Cattle needed water at the day's end and cowboys needed a personal supply while working. Containers had to be protected from damage and the sun.

Chuck box with drawers containing flour, coffee, beans, sugar, and even dried fruits

Unbreakable tin mugs for coffee

Metal hoops for canvas cover

Driver's seat

Handbrake

Bedrolls were kept in the wagon

L.L. ELLWOOD & CO.
De Kalb, Ill.
SOLE MANUFACTURERS OF THE
GLIDDEN STEEL BARB FENCE WIRE
FOR THE
WESTERN STATES & TERRIT'S

VIEW OF THE WORKS OF
WASHBURN & MOEN MANUFACTURING CO.
Worcester, Mass.
SOLE MANUFACTURERS OF THE
GLIDDEN STEEL BARB FENCE WIRE
FOR THE
EASTERN & SOUTHERN STATES

FOR SALE BY

FENCED IN
In 1874, Joseph Glidden patented barbed wire. Strong, simple, and cheap, this new type of fencing marked the end of open-range ranching. Texas cattlemen used it to enclose good pasture.

Iron-rimmed wheel

Spare rope

Water barrel

The railroad

BY THE 1850s, a railroad network covered the east and was reaching westward. Texas needed transportation links to bring in settlers and give farmers and ranchers access to eastern markets. Before the Civil War, only a few lines were completed in Texas, totaling 300 miles of track, and none connected to eastern lines. All this changed after 1865. Giant companies like Southern Pacific pushed into Texas and local lines mushroomed.

CATTLE TRAINS
The Texas cattle boom began with ranchers driving herds to the Kansas railhead towns. By the early 1880s, railroads had reached into south and west Texas, so cattle could be transported direct to the meat-packing centers such as Chicago.

EMPIRE LINE
The International-Great Northern Railroad was born out of a merger of other lines in 1873. From 1880 until the 1920s, it was part of the railroad empire founded by the famous financier Jay Gould.

NEW ORLEANS CONNECTION
The Texas & New Orleans Railroad was begun in 1856. It was reorganized in 1875, and soon connected Houston to New Orleans. In 1881, it became part of the Southern Pacific network.

DIRECT LINK
Begun in 1853, the Houston & Texas Central Railway had reached Dallas by 1872. Connecting with the Missouri–Kansas–Texas Railroad, it linked Texas directly with St. Louis, Missouri, and the east.

Protective cab for the engineer

The tender carried wood or coal for the locomotive

WORKING ON THE RAILROAD
Railroad workers graded track with picks and shovels, and laid it by spiking rails to ties with hammers. At $2 a day, they were expected to lay a mile per day – 10 spikes per rail and 40 rails per mile.

TIME TO RETIRE
Pocket watches were common until wristwatches became popular after World War I. A "one-dollar railroad watch," usually silver-plated, was often given as a retirement present to a railroad engineer or conductor.

RAILROAD FOR GROWTH
The Missouri–Kansas–Texas Railroad, nicknamed the "Katy," came south into Texas in the 1870s. Built by Civil War veterans, it brought in settlers and took out crops and cattle, helping Texas to grow.

FIT FOR THE UNITED STATES
After using British designs in the early 1800s, the United States developed its own locomotives for American conditions. This is a model of an 1875 American locomotive.

The leading truck helped the locomotive negotiate curves

The cowcatcher swept animals off the track

LUXURY TRAVEL
Operating on Southern Pacific Lines, the *Sunbeam Flyer* ran from Houston to Dallas. Its 1937 advertisement claimed it was "the smoothest running and most luxuriously furnished train in the southwest."

Black gold

IN THE EYES OF MUCH of the world, oil defines 20th-century Texas. Thanks to the hard work of Texan Pattillo Higgins, oil was struck in 1901 at Spindletop. The strike was so big it created the first oil boom. Oil dominated the Texas economy for 80 years and led to a huge petrochemical industry. Texas oil changed the world: it became the new energy source.

OIL LAKE
On January 10 1901, a wildcat driller tapped into a vast underground lake of oil at Spindletop, near Beaumont, Texas. Wells produced 17.5 million barrels in 1902.

Spindletop oilfield in 1901

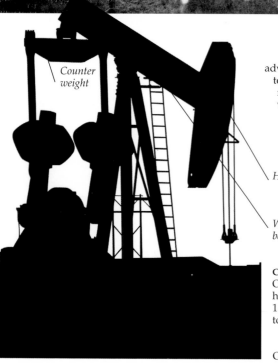

Counter weight

Horse head

Walking beam

Oil pump

FAMOUS FIREFIGHTER
Paul "Red" Adair, shown here, developed modern advanced oil disaster control techniques and became the most famous expert in the world, dealing with about 42 crises yearly.

CONTROLLING FORCES
Oil production in Texas has fallen from a peak of 1.26 billion barrels in 1972 to 379 million in 2001.

BUILT FOR STRENGTH
Offshore drilling needs platforms designed for stability and strength to resist rough weather. Most rigs rest on the seabed in shallow waters. Texas offshore rigs stretch along the Gulf Coast.

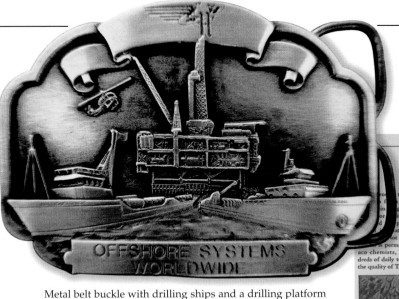

Metal belt buckle with drilling ships and a drilling platform

"If you will support my idea you will become millionaires."

PATTILLO HIGGINS
"Prophet of Spindletop"

Rotary three-cone drill bit

DRILLING FOR OIL
Possible oil reserves need exploratory drilling. Modern rotary drill bits are cooled and lubricated by a water-clay mixture, which carries the rock fragments to the surface.

EARLY EXPLORER
Texaco began in 1902 as the Texas Company. (Texaco from 1959). By 1928, it was selling in Europe, Asia, and Africa, and exploring Middle East sources from the 1930s.

Beaker of natural oil

On the long trail
with Texaco

THE TEXACO RED STAR AND GREEN T is always with you or just ahead. You are never far from that old, familiar sign.

There you can get Texaco, the volatile gas, with its pick-up, power and mileage; and Texaco, the clean, clear, golden oil— and know what you're getting.

Up and over the scenic trail through a wonderful country on a wonderful day. Texaco carries you safely and surely.

The long trail is a short trail with Texaco in the tank—and the clean, clear, golden Texaco Motor Oil in the crankcase easing the way.

THE TEXAS COMPANY, U. S. A.
Texaco Petroleum Products

TEXACO
GASOLINE — MOTOR OIL

Oil by-products
Crude oil creates more than just fuels like diesel and gasolene for vehicles, and kerosene for jet aircraft. Petrochemicals produce plastics like polyvinyl chloride and polythene, polyester and nylon for fabrics, and polishes and waxes. Ethanol is a solvent used in a range of products from paints to perfumes.

Perfume ingredients can be combined with ethanol, which then evaporates

PVC makes a waterproof raincoat

One use for oil wax is colored crayons

Texas in the 20th century

IN THE FIRST HALF of the 20th century, the United States fought two world wars, survived a major economic depression, and became the world's most powerful nation. In the next half, it built the world's most productive economy and generated vast wealth while learning to cope with old and new problems. These forces influenced life in Texas.

CHURCHMAN'S CIGARETTES

MULTI-TALENTED
Born in Houston, billionaire Howard Hughes took over the family tool company when he was 20. In the 1930s he became a movie-maker, producing and directing several famous films. He then founded Hughes Aircraft and became his own test pilot, setting several records.

HOWARD HUGHES

Side lights with kerosene lamps

Models 1913–1926 were available only in black

1914 Model T Ford

FORD COMES TO DALLAS
Henry Ford pioneered assembly-line techniques in automobile production. The famous Model T, introduced in 1909, was reliable and affordable. In addition to his Michigan plants, Ford opened a factory in Dallas in 1913.

TEXANS IN FRANCE
More than 198,000 Texans served in WWI, including 450 women nurses. The 36th "Texas" Infantry Division fought in France in the Meuse-Argonne offensive, October–November 1918, forcing a decisive German retreat and helping to end the war.

I WANT YOU FOR U.S. ARMY
NEAREST RECRUITING STATION

the original charleston

MUSIQUE DE
Cecil Mack
et
Jimmy Johnson
dansé par
Josephine Baker

DANS L'HYPER-REVUE
DES FOLIES BERGÈRE
"LA FOLIE DU JOUR"
DE LOUIS LEMARCHAND

Editions Francis Salabert
Paris . Bruxelles . New-York

ROARING TWENTIES
The 1920s saw a social revolution in America. Dance crazes like the charleston began, and there were even charleston-dancing competitions in places like Dallas.

Skull of a Texas
longhorn

DUST BOWL
Years of overcropping
followed by drought led to
terrible dust storms in 1934–35.
They blew away much of the
topsoil in Oklahoma, parts of
Kansas and Colorado, and north
Texas. Devastated farms and dead
cattle littered the Panhandle.

GREAT DEPRESSION
Ruined farmers added to city
unemployment. Shown here, Texans
in San Antonio wait patiently in line
for handouts of essential
commodities as
late as 1940.

WALL STREET CRASH
From 1927, the Wall Street stock market saw
tremendous growth. The bubble burst on
October 24, 1929. Panic set in and five days
later share values had fallen $24 billion.
Banks and stockbroking houses collapsed
and thousands of investors were ruined.

Texas movie stars

Numerous movie stars were born or brought up
in Texas. As well as Joan Crawford and Audie
Murphy, they include Ginger Rogers, Ann
Sheridan, and Jayne Mansfield. The movie
director King Vidor was born in Galveston.

*Suspension ribbon
made of silk*

Congressional
Medal of Honor

*Goddess of
War denotes
the army
medal issued
from 1904*

A NAME IN MOVIES
Joan Crawford was
born in San
Antonio. She was
one of Hollywood's
top ten stars for
many years and
won a Best Actress
Oscar for her role in
the film *Mildred
Pierce* in 1945.

Audie Murphy,
photographed in
1950

MOVIE HERO
America's most decorated soldier of WWII,
Audie Murphy was born near Kingston,
Texas. He won the Medal of Honor,
America's highest military
award, for extraordinary
bravery. He later
became a movie
star, making
44 films,
many of
them
Westerns.

Metro Goldwyn
Mayer photo of
Joan Crawford

Continued on next page

War and peace

World War II brought prosperity to Texas through war production. It continued after 1945 as aircraft, aerospace, and defense industries expanded during the Cold War. Oil prices collapsed in the post-1979 world glut. By 2000, a vast population increase and new high-technology industries gave Texas economic growth higher than the United States average.

Small helmet for confined airplane spaces

United States aircrew M4 helmet

WORLD WAR VETERAN
The battleship *U.S.S. Texas* was part of the Atlantic fleet in WWI. In WWII it supported the 1944 D-Day landings and the assaults on Iwo Jima and Okinawa in 1945. The ship is now a national memorial at the San Jacinto Monument.

Specially reinforced material

"We are going to win and we are going to win the peace that follows."

FRANKLIN D. ROOSEVELT
President of the United States

Jacket weighs 20lb

White strip introduced in 1928

United States Navy Cross

Doris Miller, Texas hero

HARBOR HERO
Doris "Dorie" Miller was born in Waco. He was a mess attendant when his ship was attacked at Pearl Harbor. He rescued wounded soldiers, then machine-gunned Japanese planes. Awarded the Navy Cross, he became an African-American hero of WWII.

United States aircrew flak jacket

SERVING THEIR COUNTRY
In WWII, three-quarters of 750,000 serving Texans were in the army and the air force. Thirty-three of them, including five Mexican-Americans, won Medals of Honor. More than 80,000 Texas African-Americans were in the services. Many United States commanders were Texas-born, including Admiral Nimitz, who commanded the Pacific Fleet from 1941.

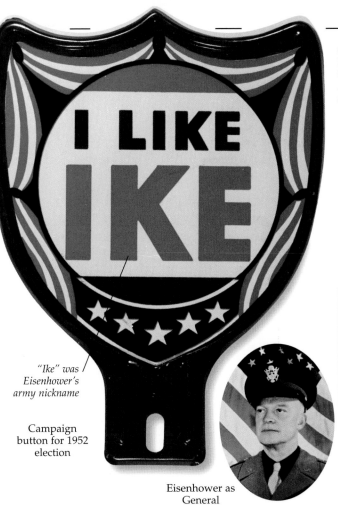

COMMANDING PRESENCE
Born in Denison, Texas, Dwight D. Eisenhower was Supreme Allied Commander for the 1944 invasion of Europe, and NATO commander 1951–52. As the Republican candidate he won the presidency in 1952 and 1956. He ended the Korean War but continued Cold War anti-Communist policies.

DEATH IN DALLAS
John F. Kennedy narrowly won the 1960 presidential election. While visiting Dallas, he was assassinated on November 22, 1963.

"Ike" was Eisenhower's army nickname

Campaign button for 1952 election

Eisenhower as General

LANDSLIDE VICTORY
Kennedy's vice-president, Lyndon B. Johnson was born in Stonewall, Texas. After succeeding Kennedy in 1963, he and Hubert Humphrey won the 1964 election by a landslide. Johnson pushed through important civil rights legislation, and launched an antipoverty Great Society program.

ELECTION SUCCESS
The Bush family moved from Connecticut to Texas in 1948 and made a fortune in oil-drilling. George W. Bush was raised in Midland, and made his career in different aspects of the oil business. He served two terms as a state governor. He was elected President in 2000, taking up office in 2001.

NEW TECHNOLOGY
Texas suffered in the 1980s oil industry decline. However, highly educated populations in cities like Houston (above), Austin, and Dallas-Fort Worth attracted high-technology companies and businesses specializing in innovation – northwest Dallas was nicknamed Silicon Prairie, a nod to Silicon Valley, California.

Farming and fishing

THE FERTILE SOIL AND warm weather make Texas ideal farming country. Almost every type of food stuff is grown here – from wheat, maize, and rice through to citrus fruits and grapes. Cotton and roses are grown too, and many different types of vegetables. Livestock, in particular beef and dairy cattle, are kept in large numbers on the many vast ranches. Offshore, in the Gulf of Mexico, fishermen catch shellfish and a wide variety of other seafood.

DRIVING TO DALLAS
During the 19th century, huge herds of cattle were driven north to railheads in Kansas or Missouri. Today, cattle are still driven to market in the major cities, notably Fort Worth and Dallas.

Hereford
bull

Hereford
cow

PRIZE HERDS
Although Texas is famed for its longhorn cattle, most of the cattle raised today are shorthorns or Herefords. These breeds are prized for their top-quality beef.

Hereford
calf

FISHY BUSINESS
The coastal city of Aransas Pass is known as the "shrimp capital of Texas." Its commercial fishing fleet brings ashore a vast quantity of shrimps. Crabs, oysters, red snappers, and flounders are also caught.

FINE WINE
The first grape vines in Texas were planted by Spanish monks near El Paso in 1662. Today, more than a million gallons of wine are produced in the 26 major vineyards in the state.

CITRUS CENTER
The lower reaches of the Rio Grande valley produce much of the citrus fruit sold in the United States. Its warm climate makes it ideal for growing grapefruit, oranges, and lemons.

Fall Creek Vineyards near Austin

"I must say as to what I have seen of Texas it is the garden spot of the world, the best land and the best prospects for health I ever saw."

DAVID CROCKETT

MIXED VEGETABLES AND FRUITS
Among the many vegetables and fruits grown in the state are carrots, potatoes, and peas. Jalapeño peppers, tomatoes, and avocados are also grown.

SUPER ONION
The Texas Super Sweet onion grows to a vast size. It is renowned for its sweet taste. It is often used to make Texan chili.

PLAIN COTTON
The plains of north and central Texas are the center of the Texan cotton industry. Lubbock County harvests more than 3 million bales of cotton per year.

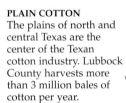

WATERED WHEAT
The area of the high plains of northwest Texas is the main producer of wheat in the state. Farmers use underground water supplies to irrigate their vast fields.

MAIZE INGREDIENT
Maize is grown across the south of the state. It is the main ingredient for making the tortilla breads and chips popular in Tex-Mex food.

BRINGING IN THE HARVEST
Harvest time used to be a labor-intensive activity, with everyone in the family required to bring in the crop. Today, combine harvesters have mechanized the job.

ROSE CAPITAL
The east Texan town of Tyler is known as the "Rose Capital of America." It grows about one-fifth of all the rose bushes sold in the country.

Food for all

THE STATE DISH of Texas is chili, a meat stew in a hot sauce of chili peppers, onions, and spices. But Texas has a wide variety of foods to eat: Tex-Mex food in the south, Cajun food such as shrimp gumbo in the east, "downhome" cooking such as chicken-fried steak in the north, and barbecues throughout the state. Immigrants from many other countries have also brought their own cuisine.

QUICK SAUCE
Supermarkets and other food shops are packed with convenience foods like this hot sauce. But you can of course make your own.

GIANT STEAKS
The Big Texan Steak Ranch in Amarillo offers a free 72oz steak if you can eat it within an hour. This is slightly heavier than the New York telephone directory!

SMOKED MEAT
When German settlers came to Texas, they brought their method of preserving meat through slow-smoking. The delicious Texas barbecue developed from this. Beef is the most popular barbecued meat, but pork is also used.

Selection of barbecue tools

"Barbecue is serious business in Texas, and it's an integral part of our state identity."

VIRGINIA B. WOOD
in the *Austin Chronicle*

Prawn

Lobster

SEAFOOD
The lakes and rivers of Texas and the Gulf of Mexico provide plenty of fish and seafood to eat. Fresh shrimp are especially popular, as are lobster, crawfish, oysters, scallops, and red snapper.

Shrimps

STRONG FLAVOR
The main flavoring used in Tex-Mex food is chili pepper. There are several varieties, such as the jalapeño, guajillo, and serrano pepper. The jalapeño is

Crushed chilis

Most chilis turn red as they mature

GOOD COMPANY
Rice is used as an accompaniment to many Tex-Mex foods. It is often mixed with small pieces of pimento – Spanish pepper.

BREAD AND CHEESE
Cornbread made from cornmeal is popular in Texas. It can be served with many foods including this *crema de queso*, or cheese soup.

BEANS ON THE SIDE
A common Tex-Mex side dish is refried beans. The beans are fried and mashed. They can be served sprinkled with cheese and herbs.

Tex-Mex food

Tex-Mex food is the Texan version of Mexican food. It is popular across the south of Texas. Its basic ingredients include cornmeal or wheat-flour tortilla breads, beans, tomatoes, onions, chili peppers, beef, and hot picante sauce.

HOT AND SPICY
Tex-Mex and Mexican curry is made with chili peppers. These small fish have been cooked in a hot chili sauce to make a spicy fish curry.

Tortilla chips

FILLED ROLLS
Enchiladas are cornmeal tortillas wrapped around a filling of meat or cheese. They are often covered with a spicy tomato sauce.

AVOCADO AND CHIPS
Guacamole is made from mashed avocado, garlic, and other seasoning. Some recipes include tomato pulp, or mayonnaise. Guacamole is often eaten with tortilla chips.

Folded tortillas

Mission Control, Houston

AFTER A ROCKET HAS blasted off into space from Cape Canaveral in Florida, attention turns toward the Lyndon B. Johnson Space Center in Houston. Here Mission Control plans, guides, and directs the flights of all United States space missions. These include the journeys of the space shuttle and the one-off satellites that explore the further reaches of the Solar System. Here, too, astronauts receive their training, and hardware is developed to keep the United States as the leader in space exploration.

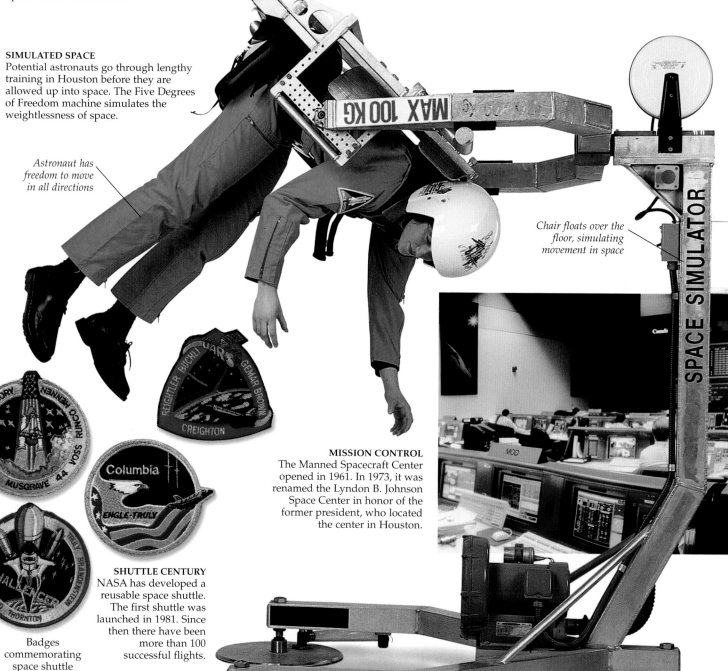

PRESIDENT'S SET-UP
The National Aeronautics and Space Administration, or NASA, was set up by President Eisenhower in 1958. NASA runs the Lyndon B. Johnson Space Center in Houston.

SIMULATED SPACE
Potential astronauts go through lengthy training in Houston before they are allowed up into space. The Five Degrees of Freedom machine simulates the weightlessness of space.

Astronaut has freedom to move in all directions

Chair floats over the floor, simulating movement in space

MISSION CONTROL
The Manned Spacecraft Center opened in 1961. In 1973, it was renamed the Lyndon B. Johnson Space Center in honor of the former president, who located the center in Houston.

Badges commemorating space shuttle missions

SHUTTLE CENTURY
NASA has developed a reusable space shuttle. The first shuttle was launched in 1981. Since then there have been more than 100 successful flights.

UNUSED ROCKET
Rocket Park outside the Space Center is full of discarded NASA hardware. The Saturn 5 rocket, built for the cancelled Apollo 18 space mission, is here.

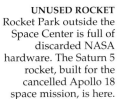

SUITABLE FOR SPACE
NASA designers have spent a huge amount of time designing spacesuits that are both safe and comfortable. William Anders wore this suit on board Apollo 8 as he orbited the Moon in 1968.

Crew worked and slept in the command module, the only part of the mission to return to Earth

MOON MISSION
In July 1969, the Space Center guided Apollo 11 to the Moon and back. As Michael Collins orbited the Moon in the Apollo capsule, Neil Armstrong and Buzz Aldrin landed the Eagle lunar module on its surface at 4.17 p.m. on July 20.

Model from Euro Space Center, Transinne, Belgium

"Houston. Tranquility base here. The Eagle has landed."

NEIL ARMSTRONG
On landing on the Moon, July 20, 1969

Multilayered pressure suit

Music and dance

TEXAS IS ONE OF the best states in the United States for music. There are many different styles to choose from – blues and country music, western swing, jazz, Spanish-influenced Tex-Mex and Tejano, French-speaking Cajun music, zydeco from Louisiana, and rock music. Many famous musicians were born and grew up in Texas, exporting their particular form of music around the world.

REVOLUTIONARY
Saxophonist Ornette Coleman was born in Fort Worth in 1930. He revolutionized jazz by introducing a new form known as free jazz. It used free personal expression.

THE SPANISH EDGE
Spanish and Mexican music are hugely popular in Texas. This mural in San Antonio shows a traditional Mexican guitarist and dancer. Other Hispanic styles of music and dance, notably Tex-Mex and Tejano, are also popular.

NEW TEJANO
The guitar- and accordion-based music known as Tex-Mex has recently evolved into a form known as Tejano. Selena Quintanilla-Perez was a successful Tejano singer. She was born in Lake Jackson in 1971.

INFLUENTIAL PLAYER
Blind Lemon Jefferson was a famous blues singer. He was born in Couchman, east Texas, on July 11, 1897. Jefferson influenced many later blues musicians with his guitar playing.

STRONG PERFORMER
Singer Janis Joplin was born in Port Arthur on January 19, 1943. Her strong voice and powerful stage presence proved that women could more than hold their own against men in rock music.

ROCK MUSICIANS
Many famous rock musicians were born in Texas, including singer Roy Orbison, the Steve Miller Band, ZZ Top, and Don Henley, main songwriter for The Eagles. Today, Austin and other large cities are home to important indie bands.

SINGING CRICKETS
Guitarist and singer Buddy Holly was born in Lubbock on September 7, 1936. In 1957 he formed the Crickets. He had international hits such as *That'll be the Day*, *Peggy Sue*, and *Oh Boy*.

SWINGING TEXAS
Texas is famous for country music, in particular the style known as Western or Texas swing. This music was first made popular by Bob Wills and his Texas Playboys.

GET ABOARD The Band Wagon

m·g·m's TOP Technicolor musical

starring CYD CHARISSE

ASTAIRE ★ CYD CHARISSE

LEVANT · NANETTE FABRAY · JACK BUCHANAN

and JAMES MITCHELL Story and Screen Play by BETTY COMDEN and ADOLPH GREEN

Songs by HOWARD DIETZ and ARTHUR SCHWARTZ

Produced by VINCENTE MINNELLI Directed by ARTHUR FREED A METRO-GOLDWYN-MAYER PICTURE

GOLD TAP
Ann Miller was born in Houston in 1923. She started her career as a tap dancer and went on to star in 40 movies and Broadway shows including *You Can't Take it with You*. These are her gold-painted tap shoes.

TALENTED STAR
The dancer Cyd Charisse was born in Amarillo in 1921. Her talent, good looks, and long legs made her a star of many movies, notably *Singin' in the Rain*, with Gene Kelly, and *The Band Wagon* with Fred Astaire.

SQUARE BUT POPULAR
A traditional cowboy dance still popular in Texas today is the square dance. Four couples form a square and swing or alternate their partners in a series of moves shouted out by a caller.

59

Good sports

TEXANS LOVE SPORTS, with thousands of them flocking to see their favorite football, basketball, hockey, or baseball teams in action. High school and college teams attract large numbers of spectators to their games, with talent scouts watching carefully to spot promising future stars. Not every athlete is as well known as Lance Armstrong, or can play as many sports as Babe Didrickson, but all are sporting stars in the eyes of their devoted Texan fans.

MULTI-SPORTSWOMAN
Born in Port Arthur, Babe Didrickson excelled at many sports. She won three athletics medals at the 1932 Olympic Games. She also won the United States Women's Golf Open three times.

Babe Didrickson at a National Amateur Golf tournament in 1946

"When a Texas team takes the field against a foreign state, it is an army with banners."

JONATHAN RABAN
Author

Football helmet

Football

Football uniform

AT THE RODEO
Rodeo is a popular spectator sport across Texas, with thousands of people cheering at such events as barrel racing (shown here), bareback riding, steer wrestling, and calf roping.

The rider has to race around and between three barrels

STATE PROFESSIONALS
Every week, thousands of people turn out to play for high school and college football teams. The state has two professional teams: the Dallas Cowboys and the newly formed Houston Texans.

60

Basketball

CHAMPIONSHIP RECORD
The Houston Comets won the Women's National Basketball Association championships for four consecutive years from 1997. Two men's teams – the Houston Rockets and the San Antonio Spurs – also have fine records.

Basketball net

FOUR TOURS
Texan Lance Armstrong won the Tour de France cycle race for the fourth year in a row in 2002. His achievement is all the more remarkable as he underwent treatment for cancer in 1997.

FAMOUS COUGAR
The famous track and field athlete Carl Lewis was a member of the Cougars of the University of Houston. He won nine Olympic gold medals including four at the 1984 Los Angeles Games.

Carl Lewis after his first gold medal for the 100m at Los Angeles, 1984

This is a beginner's bat. Bats used in major leagues are made of solid wood

MAJOR ATTRACTION
Texas has two major professional baseball teams: the Houston Astros and the Texas Rangers, as well as many college and other teams. Both teams attract huge crowds to their games.

TEXAS RANGERS BASEBALL CLUB

HOUSTON ASTROS

Baseball club patches

Ball is covered with white horsehide or cowhide

Baseball bat

Lance Armstrong at the 1996 Olympic Games in Atlanta

Baseball and glove

Celebrations

RARELY A WEEK GOES BY in Texas without a festival, a fair, or a parade to enjoy. Texans celebrate their history, folklore, and the cultures of the many different people who live in the state, as well as their ranching, farming, and of course their food. The Texas State Fair is the biggest in the country. Many towns hold their own local events, while national holidays, such as Thanksgiving and Labor Day, are also celebrated.

ON PARADE
In the third week of April, San Antonio celebrates its history with a fiesta. There are street parties, parades, dances, and other entertainments.

TURKEY DINNER
On the fourth Thursday in November, Texans, like many Americans, have a Thanksgiving supper of turkey. The Pilgrims celebrated their first successful harvest in 1621.

Big Tex is over 50ft tall

STRAWBERRY FESTIVAL
Each April the small town of Poteet, south of San Antonio, holds a celebration of its strawberry harvest. This is one of many food festivals held in Texas throughout the year.

BIG TEX
Every year for three weeks in late September and early October, Dallas hosts the Texas State Fair. The massive Big Tex cowboy statue has been the fair's symbol since the early 1950s.

TEXAS ROSE
Since 1933, the town of Tyler has held an annual rose parade and festival in mid October. All attention is focused on the Tyler Rose Queen. She is crowned in an elaborate ceremony, then a ball is held in her honor.

INDEPENDENCE DAY
Like everyone else in the United States, Texans have a national holiday on July 4 – Independence Day. This is the day on which, in 1776, the 13 colonies declared their independence from Britain.

July 4 is often celebrated with a fireworks display

OKTOBERFEST
Fredericksburg and other central Texan towns hold a festival on the first weekend of October. It is in recognition of the many German settlers who came to live here.

GRAND POW WOW
On the first weekend after Labor Day, in early September, Native Americans from across the mid- and southwest of the United States flock to Grand Prairie. They hold a pow wow to celebrate their culture.

JUNETEENTH
In the middle of June, Texans celebrate the announcement in Galveston on June 19, 1865, that slaves were free following the end of the Civil War. President Lincoln issued the original Emancipation Proclamation in 1862.

CINCO DE MAYO
On May 5, Texans commemorate the battle of Puebla in Mexico. In this battle, in 1862, the Mexicans defeated the French invasion army. Today the celebrations include plenty of Tex-Mex food.

Index

Acknowledgments

The publishers would like to thank the following for their kind permission to reproduce their photographs:

Position key: a=above; b=below; c=centre; l=left; r=right; t=top

American Museum of Natural History: 5tc, 5tr, 26c, 26tl, 26tc, 27tl, 27c. **Bridgeman Art Library**: 63bl. **British Museum**: 30tc; 39tl. **Cadbury Trebor Bassett**: 4cr. **Confederate Memorial Hall**: 38bla, 39bc. **Corbis**: 1c, 6bc, 6tl, 6cl, 7bc, 7tr, 8tr,11tc, 15tc,16tr, 17tr, 19c, 20br, 22c, 22tr, 23br, 23cl, 23tl, 23tr, 24c, 24cl, 24tr, 25bl, 27cr, 32tl, 34bc, 35br, 35tl, 37br, 39c, 42tl, 43tr, 44cr, 45br, 46bl, 47tl, 48br, 49tr, 50bc, 51bc, 52tl, 53br, 53tlb, 54tr, 57tl, 58tr, 59tc, 60tl, 61c, 61cl, 62br, 63bc, 63tl, 63tr; Austin American Statesman/Corbis 58cl; Bettmann/Corbis 2tr, 20tr, 24bc, 25br, 27bc, 27tc, 31tr, 46br, 46tc, 47cr, 49br, 50bl, 51tl, 58cr, 59tl, 59tr; David J. & Janice L. Frent Collections/Corbis 51tr, 51cr; Joseph Sohm: ChromoSohm Inc/Corbis 18tl; Lake County Museum/Corbis 14tl, 42bl, 50tl; Mosaic Images/Corbis 58tl; Stapleton Collection/Corbis 25tc. **Eurospace Centre, Transinne, Belgium**: 57cl. **H. Armstrong Roberts**: 9tc, 20cl, 35c, 51bl, 62tl. **Hulton Archive/Getty Images**: 22tl, 29bc, 30ca, 48bc, 52br, 56cr, 58c, 58bc. **Imperial War Museum**: 50tr, 50cr. **Jerry Young**: 2bl,10cr, 17br. **Mary Evans Picture Library**: 26tr, 30tr, 32cr, 32tr, 38tl. **NASA/NASA-GSFC**: 21bl. **National**

Maritime Museum: 28cl. **National Railway Museum**: 45cra. **Natural History Museum**: 2cr, 2br, 8bla, 8bl, 8cl, 8c. **NHPA**: 10c, 10cl, 12tr, 13tl, 14br, 15bl, 18cra, 19tr. **Oxford Scientific Films**: 8ca, 13cl, 17cr. **Peter Newark's Pictures**: 25c, 27br, 28bc, 28tr, 28tl, 29bl, 29tr, 31tl, 34c, 34cr, 34cl, 35cl, 35tr, 35bc, 36bla, 36tl, 37c, 38cl, 39br, 42cl, 42tr, 45cr, 49cl, 51c. **Ronald Grant Archive**: 48tr, 49bl. **Scott Foresman**: 6c, 8tl. **Science Museum**: 44bc, 57cr. **Science Photo Library/NCAR**: 20c. **Spink & Son Ltd**: 49cr. **Texas State Library & Archives Commisson**: 4cra, 36cl, 37cra, 37cr, 44cl, 44c. **Wallace Collection**: 28cr. **Warren Photographic**: 9cr. **Warwick Castle**: 29tc.

Jacket:
Chansley Entertainment Archives: Frank Driggs Collection front cra; **Corbis**: D. Boone front bc; **Christie's Images** front bl; **Darrell Gulin** front cr; **Larry Lee Photography** back tc, front tc; **DK Picture Library**: Eurospace Centre, Transinne, Belgium front c; **Hulton Archive/Getty Images**: front cr; **Oxford Scientific Films**: back cla; Royalty Free Images: **Photodisc/David Buffington** front cl.

All other images © Dorling Kindersley.